Provincelands

poems by

Maxine Susman

Finishing Line Press
Georgetown, Kentucky

Provincelands

ACKNOWLEDGMENTS

These poems have been written over many years of roaming Outer Cape Cod—
the bay and ocean beaches, marshes, woods, and dunes. My gratitude for those
welcoming, still-wild places.

Thanks to the publications where some of these poems first appeared:

Off the Coast: "Mayflower Landing, Corn Hill"
US1 Worksheets; Cool Women anthology V. 5: "Apparency," Movie Night at the Pet
Friendly Motel"
US1 Worksheets: "Fiddler Crabs"
Familiar (Finishing Line Press): "Tidal Riverbed in Spring"

I also wish to thank the Fine Arts Work Center in Provincetown, MA, where I
took workshops that led to a number of these poems. Thanks also to my critique
and performance group Cool Women, to US1 Poets, to Mark Doty, and to
Michael Klein of the Truro Center for the Arts.

Publisher: Leah Maines

Editor: Christen Kincaid

Cover Art: Maxine Susman

Author Photo: Jay Harris

Cover Design: Elizabeth Maines

Printed in the USA on acid-free paper.
Order online: www.finishinglinepress.com
also available on amazon.com

Author inquiries and mail orders:
Finishing Line Press
P. O. Box 1626
Georgetown, Kentucky 40324
U. S. A.

Table of Contents

for Jay

Movie Night at the Pet Friendly Motel

We're curled in a king-size bed
at the Outer Reach, sipping *vinho verde,*
the dog tucked somewhere in the room
as the film sprawls across Technicolor
Texas—the thirties, forties, fifties—
newlywed Liz trades Yankee gumption
for Ranch and twins, James Dean
strikes oil but Rock Hudson keeps her
though we see his range is fading—
cattle stampedes, world wars, tornado,
even a brown-skinned grandson—
two hours from the negligee scene
to man and wife parted down the middle,
skin still firm, perfect hair glued silver,
reading under separate bulbs until
lights out. "*Giant!*" you crow but PBS
cuts the credits, memory must serve.

Lucky them, I think, a lifetime together,
decades to learn who they turn into,
how things turn out, the whole panorama.
Darling, we have our own improvised screenplay—
you in your seventies, I my sixties,
up late in this enormous borrowed bed.

Return to Ballston Beach

Mindela poops, first thing.
It's good to be back.
We like it empty, early, ours. She runs off,
pushes her muzzle between the thighs
of the one other person we see,

sniffs deep, wiggles compliments,
the pretty girl gushes
Oh you adorable thing, what are you?
Ranges ahead—such smells, muck wrack ruin!

She's got my Yiddish name,
alter ego doing what a good id knows—
bark to grab attention, keep it up,
whine for what you want until you get it,
lock eyes, plead, keep wagging your tail.

I forget the human version until we're here
casing the beach, running with tails up,
tongues out. I'm getting older,
I better learn to smile a lot.

I'm glad my husband came with us,
glad he's gone home.
For two years, his blood count slipping,
I've worried until worry dug its lair.
I need to be alert, prepared,

I need to remember woman and dog,
the reliable dyad,
walking the beach with us both off-leash.
Not a dog or human
she won't make a pass at
while I call out *She's just being friendly.*

My Husband and the Seals

He's been standing for an hour,
gentle ripples rubbing at his shins,
watching a pod of seals bob and float
in the deep near waves, tossed, flipped,

their barrel bodies tumbling
in the green cylinder drum of breakers,
sometimes their heads bottling up to watch him
watch them, their bulging ponderous eyes
eye-to-eye with his—

He thinks of diving in to join them,
swimming their game, as if it could be
a kind of understanding this early in the day,
late in the season, buoyant jumble of them all.

Write a Poem about Happiness, No Abstractions

My poem of happiness begins and ends with you.

Despite that opening line you're no abstraction,
sitting bare-chested at your laptop with a diet soda,
the dog asleep under the table on your long toes
while you struggle with the wandering mouse
and your own sentences spilling their confounded
compounded meanings on the screen.
I sneak up to kiss your shoulder blade.

8:23 p.m., I'm doing 40 down Pamet Road,
the Stones throbbing on the radio, coming back
from thick mist on wet sand, the gray waves
of ocean folding into surf,
white odor of dusk wrapping beach and dunes—

is this getting abstract? Rushing back to you.

5:30 A.M.

Of course I think about death. You dying. Me. That's why

the beach. The woods. Where I don't

matter except as eye, as ear,
isolating the details—

close-up of frond, blade,
cone,

a mushroom head poking its glans
through pine needles.

Glance through pine needles up at sky.

Hours alone, the dog and eye.

Sun enough to stroke, to stoke,
to melt

what isn't calcified
as bone, shell,

shaft of feather.

Days of Awe

My mother visits me
again, as she sometimes does.
Not as she was all those years at the end,
but happy now in her unclouded mind
so I see her cleared from the fog
of my memories, the ways I wanted
not to remember.
                    She's floated free,
she comes back while the Book is open.
She's close when I stand in quiet water.
My father too, smiling, his baritone croon.

Prow

Hundreds of shipwrecks along this coast,
most never washed ashore like mine,
those curved timbers, squareheaded
brass spikes and stout wood pegs,
centuries after their pounding
into the planks still holding
some remains together,

now swallowed up
again to make me
understand
treasure.

Fiddler Crabs

We drop, the dog and I, from woods to marsh,
mid-tide, intruding on their busy village life,
crowds taking sun in front of doorway holes—
we send them scurrying, waves of creatures
rushing to their tunnels, polka dots in mudsand
running on many claws, little bellybodies
sideways, the females skittering their ballet,
males brandishing swollen claws like clubs
in threat since threatened. We Gullivers discover
more than it seems we should, their foraging hours
when tide uncovers the flux they surface for,
scudding through strands of cord grass and salt hay.
We climb back to the pitch pines, leave to them
the briny scent of slowly filling cove.

Fox Island, Low Tide

acres of oysters everywhere on the flats, wide dried
        jumble of sun-soak helter-skelter grab-hold-where-you-can—

glommed together or stuck to nubs of pebble

                        black pupils winking from insides of shells
                outsides ribbed and spiny as duck's feet

delicate eyelids of spat
        glued onto extravagant scrambled clusters

                        their comet-tails of seaweed spread on the sand.

In a few hours it all goes under—

beneath high water

down in the muck
                filtering continues

        filth and food   mouths and valves

Apparency

But I've seen the beach after a nor'easter,
what could I have expected?

No matter how far up the beach I search
one distant sandbar past another, no sign
of the broken chunk of hull,

wreck I saw once, just once,
in years of walking,

early blue low-tide morning
when I clambered over my find. Not

since. Today breakers heave
rhythm without repetition.

Fog this thick, only erasure.

Talking with My Mother

Six a.m.   I'm alone
         on a mile of sand
out of nowhere start to talk
         to myself
                  becoming my mother
talking to herself
         most of the time   no one's with her

and even when I am   if I turn my back
for a moment   she's back
         buried in her mind
talking to herself

We've returned to that Eastham rental—
         it's '93 or maybe '4—
you're not the same since Dad died—
this year barely left
         the cottage all week—

too many dogs and children—
         you wanted shade   evening ice creams

you're sitting by yourself in the other car
waiting
         to be driven away—
through the open window
         you smile   a blank smile

black chignon gone   gray hair
         half its old length
falling down your back
         Alice-in-Wonderland style

I've seen you failing
         in some ways
                  to care   who we are

                  this new person you're becoming
becoming   vaguer   clearer

I call *'Bye Mom! Love you!*

drive off with the kids
         in a different direction   leaving you
confused   where you'll be taken

now you're ninety-three
         still sometimes present
         as now with me

wind flings my words

talking out loud to you

Henry Beston's Outermost House, 1927

He builds his dune shack on the bluff
above the marsh, the edge a few feet off
with views of open sea,

walks the beach all weather, seasons,
all times of day and night, miles to town,
carrying food home in a rucksack across Nauset.

After driving an ambulance in France, Verdun,
the ocean's onslaughts, the pounding storms
and battery of gales hit pure—

not like waves of dead and dying men.
Shipwrecks on the Outer Cape claim
mere dozens at a time. A year living alone,

witnessing, then returning to his shack
to hone sentences like calligraphy
chiselled on sand when tide flows out,

a whole chapter turned over to nothing
but ocean sounds for pages and pages,
various as the flight patterns of birds.

Mayflower Landing, Corn Hill

> *"Monday, the 13th November [1620]....Our people went on shore to refresh themselves, and our women to [do the] wash, as they had great need...."*   Mourt's Relation

The Men

The ship pulls as close as sand flats allow.
Men row to shore with flaccid muscles,
hungry mouths full of God.

Some of them march off to lay their claim—
to climb, to dig, to shout their find:
a huge iron kettle, a basket "cunningly made"

and full of corn. Whose food, winter coming?
Salvation theirs by virtue
of discovery. First theft in a new place,

first of many trespasses.

The Women

Released from crammed berths
and pitching planks,
nausea, tedium, wailing, suckling,
a hold's worth of smells and stains,
the women do the wash.

They spread to the sun
the linen of rough passage
to bleach on widening sand.

Atwood-Higgins House, Built 1730

1. Guided Tour

The docent explains post and beam, beam and rafter, girt and sheathing,
who sold the property to whom when why,
but cheats us of husband, wife, children, animals—

who was born inside this blunt wood frame,
who died, who went wild, who planted roots or ran away,
shared the loft or shared a bed, how they kept clean,

how close their neighbors, how long by cart to town,
what games work lessons for the children,
what they danced and sang, took for flux and catarrh,

wore for warmth or stripped away in summer here alone,
what they ate, drank, made by hand in house and shed,
raised in garden yard barn fields stable sty,

what they found sold bought or bartered for, did without,
hauled from woods and marsh, from fresh and salt waters,
how they heard of shipwrecks, what they salvaged and brought home.

When husband and wife fought
who would submit,

did he wait longing for her,
she for him, did they go lonely

hemmed in by woods
through centuries of chores

or were they dearest friends
coming together

dappled in meadow?

2. Buttery and Keeping Room

She crosses lintel back and forth, one room
to the other, the walls smoothed with plaster
mixed of crushed oyster shells,

treading floorboards wide as the king's own masts
to beehive oven, hearth, the minister's cupboard
where spirits are kept.

Milk from the cow, potatoes from the patch,
chowder she flavors with salt scraped from eel grass,
hearing the river gurgling while she works.

Down in the cove they dig mussels, clams,
the river sends alewives flying to their nets.
Even through winter, plenty to eat.

3. Borning Room

This last time between pains I fixed the meal,

when they came strong I left the hearth
and little ones to him,

I lay down in the borning room.

We couldn't fetch the midwife through the storm.

The baby came fast, my pains were short,
this one slid right from me, lusty cries,
the afterbirth came easy this time too,

my husband cut her cord. The new one sucked
and slept. Our others came to kiss,
then played together in the keeping room.

He brought me broth from the kettle
and swaddled us snug through the February cold.

I looked out through the window giving on the river,

could almost reach my arms across the sill
to gather and hold them all.

Thoreau Walks the Outer Cape

1. Salvage

He opens with shipwreck—
an Irish hunger ship smashed on the bar,
bodies washing up along the beach
and relatives searching among them,
wagons loading paupers' coffins,
scavengers nosing for salvage—
clothing, dishes, nails clinging
to splintered boards—anything
that could be used again.

A woman keens over a narrow box.
It holds her child in her sister's arms.

2. Miles

He walks, all weather, north—
Nauset Beach to Provincetown,
Cape's elbow to forearm to tucked-under fist,

sometimes on hard-packed sand,
sometimes on the ocean-facing hills
or through thick woods and scruffy little towns.

July—his umbrella spread like a sail
pulls him all day through driving rain,

October—the dunes spread like quilts
rolling their colors to sun-dark sea.

Landlocked all his life, the better for it,
he now perceives how ocean
breathes a different soul than soil,

liquid wilderness he halts at the brink of
before hiking back up the dune.

Reading Augusta Penniman's Diary

*(With her captain husband and their son, Penniman spent the
four years of the Civil War at sea aboard the whaler Minerva.)*

She writes of Arctic regions,
stamping little ink whales on her pages
to mark species and numbers taken,
how many barrels' yield.

Before returning home they had to fill the hold.

She reads. She knits. She does the washing.
She schools her little boy, expects to earn
a hundred dollars for a year of lessons.
So she writes, but who's to pay?

Her twenty-seventh birthday spent at sea,
she notes *Did not receive any present*,

though when they come to port at Honolulu
ah, the gossip with other ladies,
the finery, finally! A new dress

before it's back to ship,
the only woman with the only child.

John Constable Paints Newcomb Hollow

Clouds, always clouds—hundreds, thousands—
      years consumed with sketching drawing painting

always sky and clouds

        each shape, each character different

                              contours of mist and air
                gather rupture lift merge swirl

toppling cumulus
                  very like a whale
but not to be
        again this way—

I cannot sometimes sight my gaze to land or waves

            when the clouds assemble their bountiful weathers

Constable would have sprawled on the ground or leaped to the dune cliff,

        tilting to frame in a vision

                              what inevitably drifts

Tidal Riverbed in Spring

When you came here
with your slit side
and missing breast
last time, to heal,
we put on old barn boots
and clambered down,
tramping the low tide muck
like kids on a dare,
not foreseeing the ordeal
of squeezing through quick-
sand, how we would sink
knee-deep in sucking tow—
the strength we'd need
to keep from drowning,
all that filth and freedom.
Today you're on the deck
looking down at the river,
not inclined this year
to make that journey,
just gazing across swamp grass
at what low tide discloses,
content now to ponder
so much rich return.

Pitch Pine at Shankpainter Pond

Three slim trunks press against each other,
conjoined triplets ratcheting up
in separate ways,
boughs crisscrossing
needles soughing

rubric of pitch pine, imprint of tree

divided to the roots.
Each torso finds
shape and form
by forming singular shape—
sprouting branches,
pushing out needles, knots and twigs,
cones and pollen,
rising slant, forked, tangled—

insisting on intransigence,
intending a design,

ponderous triplicate they dance among grasses

while inside
behind diamondback designs of bark
each trunk stores
its rings and whorls,
sap and pitch,
an inner world of wood.

Siblings bound together,
same womb, different paths.

Self-Portrait, Provincelands

*Light
is most important,* he says,
focus is least.

I'm good at composition, find what I want
and take it,
I'm sometimes patient and lucky. I slip off
the beaten path.

> Full-tide at dawn, beach with thunderheads, marsh
> oozing to half-tide, fiddler crabs hefting their tools.

Put something, he says, *up close.
A few blades of grass can render scale.
Look for a pathway leading in, a flow
pulling you inside what you see—*

> path of moonlight, trail through dune,
> sun limbering the acrobat pitch pines.

(That's my dog, romping on the sand half-way to water's edge,
she's scared of water.)

*Don't put your subject in the center,
keep it off-kilter, give it pique, tilt,
give it a kick,*

defeat expectation.
                    As we learn is bound to happen.

I'm pretty good at perspective—
long view, close-up, odd angle,
zoom or telephoto—
          lean in, squat, climb, wait—

sun-slants through slats of snow fence,
a piping plover skittering by the wrack—

What of light?
I don't know how my camera captures it,
aperture, shutter speed,
I only know to capture what I see—
sunset, waves, gulls, all the clichés without
reflection—

and focus?
Also tied to luck,
luck and adjustment yoked to perspective,
which I say I'm good at.
        But to *stay* in focus—

as one instant crashes on another,
one breaker washing in
is blown
to a ghost of white scarf, outcry of foam?

        I'm learning adjustments,
light calibrated through a shifting lens.

He says, *Find your places
and know them well. Return over and over.
They're never the same, an hour transforms them.*

We hike to Race Point Light, late August a half hour
before sunset, to catch just the right limpid bronze
as it shafts across salt hay and sculpted mud.

Come back, he says, *some day
in morning snow.*

Maxine Susman was born in Manhattan, grew up in Westchester County, NY and settled in New Jersey where she raised her son and daughter. She taught literature and writing for many years at Rutgers and Caldwell Universities, and continues to teach adult poetry classes at the Osher Institute of Rutgers. Her poems have appeared in *Paterson Literary Review, Poet Lore, Fourth River, Blueline, Ekphrasis, US1 Worksheets* and elsewhere.

In *Provincelands* and other collections she explores how and where feelings take form, sometimes in nature, sometimes in the human-made world. Her chapbook *Gogama* tells the story of her father's first job as a doctor in the bush of Northern Ontario; *Wartime Address* is about a young Brit living in Occupied France. Outer Cape Cod is the setting for many of her poems, reflecting three generations of family memories.

The Outer Cape brims with dunes, tidal marshes, pine woods, and kettle ponds. It stretches for miles of beaches on both sides, offering a natural world of great beauty, variety, and eccentricity. She and her husband now relish time at their funky little cottage near conservation lands, halfway between the bay and the ocean.

But Cape Cod is a fragile place these days, its delicate balances under siege from climate change: flooding, erosion, habitat loss. The poems in this book are offered in thanks for the Cape, and in hopes of its thoughtful preservation.

www.ingramcontent.com/pod-product-compliance
Lightning Source LLC
LaVergne TN
LVHW021124080426
835510LV00021B/3314